THE]
OUR G

HE WHO LOVES US BEST

by

Father Paul O'Sullivan, O.P.
(E.D.M.)

"Know you not, that you are the temple of God, and that the Spirit of God dwelleth in you?"
—1 Corinthians 3:16

TAN Books
An Imprint of Saint Benedict Press, LLC
Charlotte, North Carolina

ECCLESIASTICAL APPROBATION
April 25, 1952

ISBN: 978-0-89555-448-2

Library of Congress Catalog Card No.: 91-75171

Printed and bound in the United States of America.

TAN Books
An Imprint of Saint Benedict Press, LLC
Charlotte, North Carolina
2013

APOSTOLIC NUNCiATURE
LISBON, PORTUGAL

25 April 1952

Dear Father Paul O'Sullivan,

With great pleasure I have received your beautiful book on the Holy Ghost.

Really it is a new opportunity of congratulating you.

It explains in a clear and lucid way the sublime and consoling doctrine of the indwelling of the Holy Ghost in our souls, that we are, as St. Paul tells us: "Living Tabernacles of the Holy Ghost."

What joy and consolation it is for us to know that the Holy Ghost loves us so much that He dwells in our souls, not only during our lives on Earth but for all Eternity.

Your explanation of the grandeur of our souls, which God has prepared with the richest graces to be the worthy dwelling of the Third Divine Person, is most interesting and enlightening. Your appeal to Christians to love and pray to the Holy Ghost is irresistible, for you show what helps, joys and consolations those receive who honor the Holy Spirit and what those lose who so ungratefully forget and neglect their Divine Guest.

The pages of your book are full of interesting and useful information, which will be a surprise to many who know so little about the Gifts, the Beatitudes and the Fruits of the Holy Ghost. It will be an incentive to priests and teachers to make the Holy Ghost better known to the faithful.

I recommend this little but important book most heartily, feeling sure that it will cause a great increase of devotion to the Holy Spirit.

Cordially blessing you, I am

Yours sincerely,

✢ P. CIRIACI, *Papal Nuncio*

Contents

Foreword

Our Greatest Friend! Never has a title been better deserved.

This little book makes known to its readers their greatest, truest, best Friend, a Friend who can and will give them what all so earnestly desire—peace, happiness and joy.

Can this be possible? Read, Dear Friend, and judge for yourself. No wonder that you are incredulous. You have never known this Friend.

Who is He? He is the Holy Ghost, the Third Divine Person of the Blessed Trinity, who is in your soul personally, really and truly as He is in Heaven. He is your dearest, most intimate, most loving Friend. He is in your soul, but before coming into it He has made it worthy of His Divine Presence. He has lavished on it His choicest gifts and graces and made it so beautiful that, were you to see it, you would die of love.

Dear Friend, all this seems incredible to you. Have you never heard about it before? Pope St. Leo tells you: "Christian, recognize your divine rank, your dignity."

It is incredible that all this is true and yet you never knew it!

Read carefully these pages once and many times. They will tell you how to honor and love your Divine Guest, who in return will bestow on you His seven Gifts, His Beatitudes and His Fruits.

Henceforth your life will be holy, full of the peace, the joys and consolations which the Holy Spirit gives to all who love Him.

Chapter 1

The Importance of Devotion To the Holy Ghost

The following pages will, we hope, dear Reader, prove to be the most interesting and useful you have ever read. They will tell you all about the Holy Ghost, about whom you possibly know very little.

The doctrine of the Holy Ghost is without doubt the most important of all the Church's teachings because, if we do not know and love the Holy Ghost, we cannot possibly understand the other great truths of our Holy Religion.

Without the Holy Ghost we are blind.

Not only is this doctrine the most important, it is the most wonderful, the most consoling, the most sublime of all doctrines, for with the Holy Ghost we can do all things easily and well. He is the Spirit of Love, of Peace, of Joy, the Spirit of Divine Consolation. He is the Light of Our Souls and the Strength of Our Wills.

Yet, strange to say, this doctrine is little understood by great numbers of Christians. Some have a vague knowledge of the Holy Ghost, but very few indeed have a real grasp of all the Holy Ghost has done for them and is most ready to do if only they allow Him.

We love and honor the Eternal Father whenever we say the *Our Father*, and this not once, but many times a day. Whenever, too, we speak of the Great Creator of Heaven and Earth, the God of the Universe, we think of the Eternal Father.

We pray to the Son, not only when invoking the Blessed Trinity, but when praying to Our Lord Jesus Christ. We honor His Incarnation, His life, His Passion and death. We honor His Sacred Heart, His Holy Name, and above all we honor Him in the Holy Eucharist.

But many rarely or ever think of the Holy Ghost! They know very little about all the wonderful things He is ready to give them—the peace, the immense joy, the consolations, the love He is offering them.

"*How extraordinary*," **Cardinal Manning** exclaims, "it is that Christians know so little about the Holy Ghost though He is the Author of our Sanctification, the Giver of all Joys and Consolations!"

His Eminence was in his youth a sincere Protestant. He became, with the help of the Holy Ghost, a fervent Catholic.

Under the same divine guidance, he became a priest, a bishop and finally a cardinal.

He ever cherished a great devotion to the Holy Ghost and solved all his doubts and difficulties by praying to this Holy Spirit.

When called on to make any important decision, he first of all bent his head in silent prayer. If the problem were graver, he devoted more time and fervor in asking for guidance. Thanks to the graces he thus received, he was able not only to attain high personal sanctity but to render great services to the Catholic Church in England. He wrote two beautiful books on the Holy Ghost.

Cardinal Newman gives us a touching example of love for the Holy Ghost.

He, too, was brought up by his parents in the Protestant religion. Unfortunately, he had the strongest prejudices against the Catholic Church.

At an early age he began to see that his own religion could not be the true one, so full was it of contradictions and errors.

He spent years trying to find the Church of Christ. He read history, he argued with eminent divines and consulted many learned friends, but all in vain. He failed to recognize in the midst of so many claims the religion given us by Jesus Christ.

Finally, one day he received from God, who was pleased with his good intentions, an inspiration.

"What have I been doing!" he exclaimed. "I have labored much, I have studied, I have read many books, I have consulted good friends, but I have not prayed enough, I have not sufficiently asked God's light and guidance."

Then falling on his knees he prayed fervently. The clouds of doubt began to disappear, and he at last saw the truth of the Catholic Church.

He describes his conversion in the following beautiful hymn, written not long before his conversion.

Lead Kindly Light

Lead Kindly Light, amid the encircling gloom,
      Lead Thou me on!
The night is dark, and I am far from home—
      Lead Thou me on!
   Keep Thou my feet; I do not ask to see
   The distant scene—one step enough for me.

I was not ever thus, nor pray'd that Thou
      Shouldst lead me on,
I loved to choose and see my path; but now
      Lead Thou me on!
I loved the garish day, and, spite of fears,
      Pride ruled my will:
      remember not past years.

So long Thy power hath blest me, sure it still
      Will lead me on,
O'er moor and fen, o'er crag and torrent, till
      The night is gone;
And with the morn those angel faces smile
      Which I have loved long
      since and lost awhile.

He became a Catholic, and following his example, more than a thousand Protestant ministers were converted and a very host of laymen.

Cardinal Gibbons had the following experience when still a parish priest: He was called to see a distinguished American senator who was gravely ill. Unfortunately, the sick man did not believe in the existence of God. He listened, however, attentively to Father Gibbons, who spoke to him of the goodness of God and His love for us, proving at the same time God's existence with several cogent arguments. These, however, made no impression on the Senator.

Father Gibbons finally asked him whether, if such a good God as he had been describing did exist, he would believe in and love Him? "Most certainly," was the answer.

"Well then," said Fr. Gibbons, "will you say the following little prayer sometimes: 'O God of infinite goodness, if You exist, make me know You.'"

This the sick man promised to do, and then came a flood of light!

Some days after, Fr. Gibbons was once more summoned to the bedside of the dying man, who on seeing him, called out, "Father, I believe, I believe!" And for the remaining weeks of his life he manifested the liveliest faith in and love for God.

A priest who is devoted to the Holy Ghost does more than a thousand others. The writer met one such priest recently. He was extremely modest and unpretentious, yet he got through a prodigious amount of work.

He not only worked successfully himself, but he

had the gift of attracting and inspiring others to work with him.

In the course of conversation he mentioned that he had great devotion to the Holy Ghost, to whom he attributed all his success.

When Catholic universities commence the year's work, when law courts begin their annual sessions, at the opening of parliaments and other important corporations, the Mass of the Holy Ghost is solemnly said and His Divine guidance invoked, and as we shall see afterwards, individual members of these corporations beg light and help from the Holy Ghost in all grave emergencies.

We, too, should make it our practice to seek in all things the guidance of the Holy Spirit.

Chapter 2

The Holy Ghost and What He Does for Us

What is this wonderful doctrine of the Holy Ghost?

The Holy Ghost is the Third Person of the Holy Trinity, equal in every way to the Father and to the Son and equally deserving of love and adoration.

This is about all that many Christians know of the Holy Ghost. But what He is to us, what He does for us, and what He wishes to do for us, few understand.

What the Holy Ghost Does for Us

The first all-important fact that we must fully understand is that the Holy Ghost is really, truly and *personally* in our souls even as He is in Heaven. He loves us with a most tender and infinite love and earnestly desires to pour out on us His Gifts and graces. This He cannot do if we do not correspond to His love, if we do not know Him, love Him and pray to Him.

Our most grave obligation, then, is to bear clearly in mind and fully realize that the Holy Ghost is in us, and not merely by His graces and Gifts, but *personally* and as really as Jesus Christ is in the Tabernacle, though in a different way.

Every soul in the state of grace is a living tabernacle of the Holy Ghost, and as we are obliged to adore and honor Jesus Christ on the altar, so too are we obliged to honor the Holy Ghost in our souls.

The Presence of Our Lord in the Blessed Sacrament in millions and millions of Sacred Hosts in the cities and towns of the whole world, and even in the wild deserts of Africa and Asia, day and night, is indeed a proof of the boundless love of God for us. But the Presence of the Holy Ghost in our souls is still more amazing, because God's Presence in the Blessed Sacrament will cease on the last day; whereas, the presence of the Holy Ghost in our souls will never cease. It will last for all Eternity.

Moreover, Our Lord in the Blessed Sacrament is on the altar; whereas, the Holy Ghost is in our very souls.

St. Paul says, "Know you not, that you are the temple of God, and that the Spirit of God dwelleth in you?" (*1 Cor.* 3:16).

And again: "Your members are the temple of the Holy Ghost, who is in you, whom you have from God." (*1 Cor.* 6:19).

And St. John: "And I will ask the Father, and he shall give you another Paraclete, that he may abide with you for ever. The spirit of truth, whom the world cannot receive, because it seeth him not, nor knoweth him: but you shall know him; because he shall abide with you, and shall be in you." (*John* 14:16–17).

The Saints and the Holy Ghost

All the Saints were filled with the Holy Ghost. Their souls overflowed with joy and consolation. They did all the wonders we read of in their lives by the help of the Holy Ghost. With the strength He gave them, all sufferings were easily borne and all difficulties overcome.

St. Ignatius Martyr (of Antioch), who was insulted by the Emperor Trajan because he was a Christian, replied, "Do not insult Ignatius the God-bearer."

Trajan demanded, "Why do you say that you are the God-bearer?" "Because," answered Ignatius, "it is true, God is in me."

When **Origen** was a child, his father, Leonidas, used to kneel by his bedside when he was asleep and kiss his breast because the Holy Ghost was in his soul.

When the same Origen became one of the most learned Fathers of the Church, he used to say: "Our souls are little heavens because God is really in them."

St. Cyril: "The Holy Ghost impresses on us the divine image and gives us superhuman loveliness. We are temples of the Holy Spirit, who truly lives in us. On this account we are called gods. Because of our union with the Holy Ghost, we share the divine, incomprehensible nature of God." (St. Cyril, *Dial. VII*).

Again, the same Saint says, "We have not merely the enlightenment of the Holy Ghost, but He Himself dwells in us." "Man is composed of a body and soul and the Holy Ghost."

St. Basil: "By the Holy Spirit each of the Saints is made divine, as God Himself has declared, 'I have said you are gods.'" (St. Basil, *Con Eunom.*).

Cornelius a Lapide says, "When the soul enters our bodies, it gives them light and life, which they had not before; so also, when the Holy Ghost comes into our souls, He gives them a new life, His own life, He deifies them."

Another of the Holy Fathers says, "The Holy Ghost is not in our souls as a guest. He is there as a bridegroom, for His union with us is a marriage; it is a most intimate and loving union."

The Holy Ghost said to **St. Angela:** "I am the Holy Ghost who has come to thee and will give thee such a joy as thou never yet tasted. I accompany thee, I am present in thee. Thou art My spouse, I will never leave thee."

"Hearing these words," the Saint said, "I cannot describe the joy I then felt."

His Angel Guardian once said to **Blessed Henry Suso,** "Fix your eyes on your breast." Bl. Henry did so and his body became transparent and he saw God in his soul.

Our Lord said to **St. Catherine of Siena,** "Contemplate Me in your soul, and you shall know that I am your Creator."

St. Teresa of Jesus says, "Our soul is a little heaven in which the Creator of Heaven and Earth takes up His abode. Is there anything so grand as to see Him, whose grandeur would fill a thousand worlds, hiding Himself in such a little dwelling as our soul!"

St. Philip Neri, when once begging God to give him the Holy Ghost, saw a globe of fire which entered his mouth and passed into his breast. The heat that it caused was so great that he lay prostrate on the ground and tore open his habit. He felt a wondrous joy fill his soul. His heart was greatly enlarged, and two of his ribs remained broken so that his heart could beat without difficulty. He felt no pain, but when saying Mass or giving Holy Communion, his joy was so great that his whole body shook and made the altar shake. Sometimes he cried out, "I cannot bear such joy! Stop, Lord, or I shall die!"

The holy Curé d'Ars said, "Those who love the Holy Ghost experience every kind of happiness within themselves. The Holy Ghost leads us like a mother leads her little child, or like a person with sight leads a blind man. Those who love the Holy Ghost find prayer so delightful that they cannot find sufficient time to pray."

The Breton poet **Botrel** had once to take an oath in court. There was no crucifix there which he could hold when swearing, so he placed his hand on his breast and said, "God is here; by Him I swear."

A French officer, a brave soldier and a fervent Catholic, was imprisoned in the fortress of Lille because he refused to obey an order to carry out persecution against the Church. He found immense delight and consolation in adoring the Holy Ghost in his soul. "He is here. He is with me. I am His tabernacle," he used to say.

Pope Alexander had an intense devotion to Our Lord in the Blessed Eucharist, and to satisfy this great love, he caused to be made a beautiful golden pyx in which he placed the Blessed Sacrament every morning and wore it on his breast during the day. This perpetual adoration obtained for the Holy Pontiff the greatest graces and consolations. He felt that he was always in the presence of Our Lord.

Now each one of us [in the state of Sanctifying Grace] carries the Holy Ghost Himself in us—not in a golden pyx on our breast, but in our very souls.

What an immense joy and consolation for those who realize this wonderful fact!

Dear Reader, ask yourself if you realize it. Do you believe that the Holy Ghost is really in your soul; do you adore and love Him?

Chapter 3

The Holy Ghost Comes into Our Souls in Baptism

The Holy Ghost comes into our souls in Baptism. He remains there forever. Day and night we carry Him about in our souls. Wherever we go, whatever we are doing, the Holy Ghost is really and truly with us. He only leaves us if we commit a mortal sin. By a deliberate mortal sin—oh, horror of horrors—we expel Him from our souls with all His Divine love and graces. In His place the devil comes and fills that glorious soul with all the horrible corruption and filth of Hell.

If such an awful thing happens to any of us, let us throw ourselves on our knees and beg God's pardon and go to Confession.

When our souls are washed in the Precious Blood of Jesus Christ, the Holy Ghost will once again return to the soul, which He so tenderly loves and will once more fix His abode in it.

How Long Does the Holy Ghost Remain in Our Souls?

He remains in our souls not only during all our life, but during all eternity, forever and forever.

As we have said, we are bound to love and adore Him in our souls as really and truly as we are bound to adore Jesus Christ on the Altar.

Nay, more; as an eminent Dominican theologian remarks, we have in a way a greater obligation to adore the Holy Ghost in our souls than to adore Jesus Christ on the altar, because if we fail to honor Jesus Christ on the altar, many others who enter the church will adore Him, so that He will not be abandoned and left alone. But if we fail to adore, honor and love the Holy Ghost in our souls, He is completely abandoned and left alone. No one can take our place. This is our personal obligation.

What an immense joy and consolation it is, we repeat, for us to know that the Holy Ghost is really, truly and *personally* in our souls. We are His living tabernacles. He is always with us. It seems incredible that few Christians realize this wonderful truth. They never think of the Holy Ghost during the long hours of the day; much less do they honor Him during the night, during their seven or eight hours' sleep.

But how can they honor the Holy Ghost when they are asleep? By realizing that He is with them when asleep and by offering their sleep in His honor, as we shall explain later on.

What a joy it would be to them if at night when they awaken, and sometimes when they remain awake for hours at a time, they spoke lovingly to Him and enjoyed His presence.

And again how consoling for the sick, when suffering and alone, if they felt that the Holy Ghost Himself was really and truly with them. They never perhaps heard of this beautiful doctrine.

Many Christians never even address a single word, a single tiny prayer to the Divine Spirit. They seem to be utterly ignorant that He is in their souls. They make absolutely no account of Him.

This goes on day after day, all their life long!

Chapter 4

The Exceeding Beauty of Our Souls, Made Worthy to Receive the Holy Ghost

That we may the better realize this divine truth, let us see with what care God has prepared our souls to be the worthy tabernacles of the Holy Ghost. Many Christians too have little idea of the greatness and grandeur of their souls.

We are composed of a body and soul. Our bodies are clay and into clay they return after death. Whatever beauty they have comes from the soul. Our souls are immortal, like to God Himself.

Yet men, as an almost universal rule, give most attention to the care, the welfare, the happiness of their poor bodies. In every 24 hours, their main concern is for the needs, the comforts of these bodies.

They rest them by long hours of sleep; they eat abundantly to nourish them; they give them every possible pleasure. If these bodies suffer the slightest pain or discomfort, they hasten to relieve it. They call doctors and use expensive remedies.

But in all the 24 hours of the day, many think little or nothing at all of their souls.

What Does God Think of Our Souls?

Now let us see the immense value that our souls have in the eyes of God—the care, the love with which God has made them, how He has expended all the riches of His wisdom and power in adorning them and making them worthy residences of the Holy Ghost.

Thus perhaps we shall more easily understand why it is that the Holy Ghost resides in us.

Our Creation

One of the first questions of the Catechism is, "Who made you?" The answer is, "God made me." These few words do not impress us; they are not sufficiently explained to us, and as a consequence, few people have the faintest idea of the wonders of their creation. They never think of thanking God for all that He has done for them when bringing them into being.

Instead of me, He might with the same facility have created a great saint or a glorious angel. Why did He create poor me? Because He loved me with an infinite love.

Let us pause to meditate on this first immense proof of God's love for us.

Our Soul, God's Masterpiece

God Himself created us with His own "divine hands." He created us simply because He loved us. He made us to His perfect image and likeness. He did not create us as He created others of His creatures. He created us with a special love. He created us as His own dear children, children who will be His forever and forever, children who will be with Him for all eternity, seated on glorious thrones in His presence, enjoying His happiness and sharing in His glory.

In creating us, He used His infinite wisdom, His infinite power, His infinite love, His infinite generosity in making us to His own perfect image and likeness.

Our likeness to God is not a merely external appearance; it is in the very essence of our being. He made our souls spirits like Himself; He made our souls immortal like Himself. Our souls will live as long as God lives.

He gave us faculties like His very own. He gave us a glorious intelligence like His divine intelligence. He gave us a free will, independence in our actions, a will that nothing can coerce, a will so wonderful that, if we only use it rightly, its every act will have an eternal reward. He gave us the power of looking at the past, the present and the future, as He Himself does.

The soul of man, thus formed and fashioned by God, is the most wondrous thing in creation.

Our Soul Like to God Himself

His Divine Goodness was not yet satisfied with all the natural gifts He had given us. He resolved to raise us by a new and still more wonderful creation to a divine rank. He made us as gods. (St. Thomas Aquinas).

In the words of the Apostle **St. Peter,** He gave us a real participation of His own divine nature. (*2 Peter* 1:4). This sanctifying grace, this divine life, He pours into the substance of our souls, and thence into our faculties, making them capable of the highest supernatural acts.

Looking on us thus radiant, thus transfigured by this divine beauty, He can well exclaim: "What could I do for My vineyard that I have not done." He made us, indeed, the masterpiece of His divine hands.

St. John Chrysostom says that, before we receive the Holy Ghost, we are like a man weighed down with age and infirmities, but when the Holy Ghost comes into us, we are made young, beautiful and full of energy.

Blosius says that, did we see our souls in the state of grace, we should be transported with joy and delight.

St. Mary Magdalen de Pazzi says that we should die of love did we see the beauty of our souls.

God Himself Watches over Us

One of the most beautiful and touching proofs of the love that God gives us is His personal care of each one of us. Since the moment of our creation, He has never taken His eyes off us. Nothing happens to us, not the least thing, without His divine consent. "Not a hair falls from our heads without His knowledge or permission."

We are touched when we see the tender care and watchfulness of a mother who has her eyes ever on her little child, making sure that no evil happens to it.

The mother's care gives us but the faintest idea of God's sweet care of each one of us.

As we saw, God gave us all His love and attention at the moment of our creation. This love and care has not ceased or diminished for one instant in all those long years of our life.

How little we prize this most tender and infinite love of God for us!

Still Another Proof of God's Love

At the moment we came into the world, God called one of His great princes, a glorious angel, and bade him guard and guide us. He bade him devote all his angelic power, all his wisdom and love to helping us, to keeping us from harm and defending us against all dangers.

This Angel loves us with unspeakably great love,

first of all because God has given us to his care; secondly, because he loves us himself with all the strength and love of his angelic nature; thirdly, because we are in ourselves things so surpassingly lovely.

We wonder, in reading the story of Tobias, when we see how good God was to send him the Angel Raphael to accompany him on his journey and obtain for him many great benefits. Much more should we wonder that each one of us has a glorious Angel as companion, not for a week or a month, but for all our lives, an Angel who gives us all his care. He never leaves us; he obtains for us all kinds of graces and saves us from countless dangers.

It is because our souls are so perfect, so dear to Him that God gives us this Angel all to ourselves, to protect us, to help us, to love us.

Yet many Christians do not realize the favor God has done them in giving them this glorious Angel to watch over them. They never thank their Angel for all he is ever doing for them, nor for the dangers he saves them from, nor do they call on him for the help which he is only too ready to give them in their difficulties.

Chapter 5

The Holy Ghost Is Personally In Our Souls

Now that God has made the soul perfect with all these gifts of nature and grace and that it is indeed a worthy tabernacle for the Third Divine Person, the Holy Ghost then comes into it with ineffable love and makes it His living Tabernacle forever.

The Seven Gifts

He pours out on it His gifts and graces and infuses into it the theological virtues of Faith, Hope and Charity; He gives us His Seven Gifts, which help us to follow His inspirations and which strengthen our natural powers so that we see better and act with more strength. These Gifts are **Knowledge**, **Understanding**, **Wisdom** and **Counsel**, which enlighten and help the intelligence, and **Fortitude**, **Piety** and **Fear of the Lord**, which strengthen our wills.

The Gift of **Wisdom** helps us to think less of worldly things and more of God and our spiritual life.

The Gift of **Understanding** helps us to grasp and realize heavenly truths.

The Gift of **Counsel** is what we may call divine prudence, which enables us to choose what is pleasing to God and good for ourselves.

The Gift of **Fortitude** gives us strength to do our duties well.

The Gift of **Knowledge** helps us to see and avoid dangers to our soul and our spiritual welfare.

The Gift of **Piety** helps us to love God more tenderly, with more confidence, and to do everything lovingly for Him.

The Gift of **Fear of the Lord** inspires us with reverence and respect for God and all things relating to Him and inspires us with a filial fear of giving Him offense.

These are called "Gifts" because we do not acquire or merit them. They are given us freely by the Holy Ghost. When we obey and follow the inspirations they give us, we receive the Beatitudes, that is, new ideas, new views, new activities, a new life. We become more meek, more joyful, more peaceful and more clean of heart.

The Eight Beatitudes

1. Blessed are the poor in spirit, for theirs is the Kingdom of Heaven.
2. Blessed are the meek, for they shall possess the land.
3. Blessed are they that mourn, for they shall be comforted.

4. Blessed are they that hunger and thirst after justice, for they shall have their fill.
5. Blessed are the merciful, for they shall obtain mercy.
6. Blessed are the clean of heart, for they shall see God.
7. Blessed are the peacemakers, for they shall be called the children of God.
8. Blessed are they that suffer persecution for justice' sake, for theirs is the Kingdom of Heaven.

What wonderful graces the Holy Ghost gives us, if only we ask Him.

The Fruits of the Holy Ghost

From the Gifts and the Beatitudes flow the Fruits of the Holy Ghost, which are **Joy**, **Patience**, **Mildness**, **Benignity**, **Modesty**, **Chastity** and other like graces [or virtues]. They are all those acts we do with peace, pleasure, joy and love. (St. Thomas Aquinas).

These graces are called "Fruits" because they are the crowning favors, the result of all the Holy Spirit has been doing for us. They are to our souls what the fruit is to the tree, what the flower is to the plant.

We thus become an object of delight to the Father and the Son, who come too and dwell in our souls, which thus become the home of the Blessed Trinity.

These Gifts, Beatitudes and Fruits we receive by

prayer and good works, by Holy Mass, Communion and the Sacraments. Strange that many Christians never think of asking for the Gifts, the Beatitudes, the Fruits of the Holy Ghost.

These Gifts and graces do not make our lives sad or austere.

Far from it, they fill us with a peace, a joy, and a consolation we never felt before. What was before difficult to us becomes now easy and delightful, for the Holy Ghost, as we have said, is the Spirit of joy, peace and consolation. He enlightens, He strengthens us, He enables us to know God as we never knew Him before. He gives us a foretaste of Heaven.

Joy and consolation are in fact the chief characteristics of the Holy Ghost. Thus we read in the Acts of the Apostles, "The disciples were filled with joy and the Holy Ghost."

St. Paul says, "I superabound in joy in all my tribulations."

Joy is a result of holiness, and we find the Saints the most joyful of mortals. St. Dominic, for instance, was always most joyful. He was never sad, except when he heard of the sorrow of others.

Charismata

There are other Gifts called "charismata," which are not given to sanctify the person who receives them, but are given for the help and benefit of others. Such are the gifts of working miracles, healing the sick, the gift of tongues, the gift of prophecy—all of which are given when necessary.

It is well to remark that we sometimes attribute to one or other of the Divine Persons works or perfections which in reality are common to all the Divine Persons. We do this by what theologians call appropriation, that is, because these perfections seem to be more connected with the personal characteristics of that Divine Person. We attribute Power and the work of Creation to the Father, because He is the Principle of the Son and Holy Ghost. We attribute Wisdom to the Son, because He proceeds from the Father by the intellect. We attribute the sanctification of souls, the Gifts and Fruits to the Holy Ghost, because He proceeds from the Father and the Son by Their mutual love.

Chapter 6

How Are We to Honor the Holy Ghost in Our Souls?

If the Holy Ghost is, as we have said, really in our souls, loving us with an unspeakably great love and craving for our love in return, we must above all realize and remember His Divine Presence. We must not, as many do, pass the whole day, pass many days and weeks in complete forgetfulness of Him.

True, we cannot be praying constantly to Him all day long, but we can honor and adore Him in many different ways:

First, by offering to Him our daily prayers, Masses, Communions and good works.

We increase the Gifts and graces of the Holy Ghost by prayer and the reception of the Sacraments.

Second, by offering in His honor all the actions of the day. We can offer Him our daily work, our sleep, our eating, all we do, as St. Paul tells us: "Whatever you do in word or work, do all in the name of Our Lord Jesus Christ." The Apostle continues: "Whether you eat or drink or *whatever else* you do, do all in the name of Our Lord Jesus Christ."

27

We thus honor the Holy Ghost day and night by offering for love of Him all we do. It is He who commands us to eat, to sleep, to work, to rest. Surely there is no difficulty in doing all this for the love of Him.

Third, by saying special prayers to the Holy Ghost. We daily say these prayers to the Holy Ghost, but we do not always give them sufficient attention.

Every time we make **the Sign of the Cross**, we say: "In the Name of the Father, and of the Son, and *of the Holy Ghost*." In the future, when repeating these words, let us say with special emphasis the words, "*Holy Ghost*," not that we wish to give more honor to the Holy Ghost than to the Father and the Son, but only that we may make reparation to Him for our past neglect.

The same applies to another prayer we repeat so often, *viz.*: **"Glory be** to the Father and to the Son and *to the Holy Ghost*." We say this beautiful prayer very frequently, but many say it without due attention. Let us try for the future to emphasize a little the words "to the Holy Ghost." This prayer, said once with devotion, is worth more than the same prayer said a thousand times hastily and irreverently.

A third special prayer in honor of the Holy Ghost is the **Third Glorious Mystery** of the Rosary, *viz.*, "The Descent of the Holy Ghost on Our Lady and the Apostles."

It should be clearly our intention when saying this mystery to ask God's sweet Mother and the

Apostles to obtain for us all the Gifts and graces of the Holy Ghost, as they received them on the Feast of Pentecost.

Remark that these three prayers are no additional burden, for we are already accustomed to say them frequently. Only, for the future, let us say them more devoutly.

Fourth, by ejaculatory prayers to the Holy Ghost.

"Holy Ghost, God of Love, I adore Thee really and truly in my soul. Oh, give me Thy holy love."

"Holy Ghost, God of Peace, really and truly in my soul, give me Thy blessed peace, which surpasses all understanding."

"Holy Ghost, God of Light, really and truly in my soul, give me Thy blessed light, that I may see all things clearly."

"Holy Ghost, God of Joy and Consolation, really and truly in my soul, fill me with Thy joy and consolations."

"Holy Ghost, God of Strength, really and truly in my soul, give me Thy divine strength, that I may do all things well."

"Holy Ghost, God of infinite Sweetness and Goodness, really and truly in my soul, give me Thy seven Gifts, Thy Beatitudes and Fruits."

We can say these ejaculations, some or all of them, at night when we awake or during the day when working or at any time. They will keep us ever in the blessed presence of the Holy Ghost and will bring us joy and consolation.

Fifth, by the practice of virtues.

All virtues please the Holy Ghost, but two attract Him most especially, *viz.*, *humility* and *purity*. We should therefore use diligent care in cultivating these virtues and avoiding faults of pride, vanity and impurity.

Our Duty Toward Ourselves and Others

Since the Holy Ghost is really in us, we must respect ourselves. At High Mass the celebrant is incensed, then the deacon and subdeacon, and then all the people. Why? Because the Holy Ghost is in them. Incense is offered to God.

For the same reason we must respect and honor others. If we offend, insult or injure others, if we speak badly of them, we are offending not only their angel guardians, but far more, the Holy Ghost Himself.

This is especially so if we hurt or harm children. The greatest reverence is due to little ones.

The Holy Ghost is in our souls, and because our souls are so intimately united with our bodies, He is also in our bodies. "Know you not, that your members are the temple of the Holy Ghost, who is in you." (*1 Cor.* 6:19).

Therefore, we must respect our bodies, avoiding especially faults of modesty when dressing or washing.

The Church commands us to honor even the bodies of the dead because they had once been the temples of the Holy Ghost.

After death the dead are taken to the church and there sprinkled with holy water and incensed. They are then buried in a consecrated, or at least in a blessed, cemetery.

Catholic cemeteries should be carefully kept, firstly, because we must show love and respect for our dear departed ones; secondly, because their bodies, which lie here, were temples of the Holy Ghost; thirdly, because the cemeteries themselves are solemnly consecrated, even as churches are, and may be easily desecrated.

Sometimes cemeteries are allowed to fall into a disgraceful state of neglect, which is an offense to the Holy Ghost and to our dead.

It is a commendable custom to visit the graves of our friends, and when we pass cemeteries, we should salute them as we do churches and say a little prayer for those buried in them.

The Church manifests in many ways her wish that we honor the Holy Ghost:

First, by the great Feast of Pentecost, when we commemorate the Descent of the Holy Ghost on Our Blessed Lady and the Apostles. This feast is celebrated with the greatest liturgical pomp and is followed by a most solemn octave. Plus, the 24 Sundays after the Feast are called the "Sundays after Pentecost."

Second, the faithful are invited to honor the Holy

Ghost on the Mondays of every week.

Third, the whole month of April is dedicated to the Holy Ghost, as the month of June is to the Sacred Heart.

Fourth, the Holy Ghost is fervently invoked in the celebration of the Sacraments.

The Holy Ghost protects, guides and directs the Church of Christ, so that the gates of Hell will never prevail against it.

He not only protects the Church, but He dwells also in all her members.

The Holy Ghost speaks to us in the Sacred Scriptures, of which He is the principal Author. It was He, too, who inspired and spoke through the Prophets.

Therefore, the Church wishes us to read the Sacred Scriptures, the greatest and holiest of all books, the word of God Himself.

Chapter 7

With the Holy Ghost We Can Do All Things

The Apostles

We have a very clear example of the action of the Holy Ghost on our minds and hearts in the story of the Apostles.

Our Lord chose twelve weak, rude, ignorant men for His Apostles. They were not only rude and ignorant, but they were timid and fearful. He chose them expressly that they might be an example and encouragement to us, an example that the weakest of us can follow.

For three whole years they were in the constant company of Our Lord, hearing His beautiful doctrine, seeing the marvels He wrought, listening to His words of comfort and consolation.

Yet, for all that, they remained dull of comprehension. They did not grasp His teaching; they did not understand and realize the wonderful doctrines He taught and the promises He made.

Once He said to **Philip**, "Philip, how long have I been with you and yet you do not know Me."

Once, too, He addressed that severe rebuke to

Peter, "Get behind Me, Satan," because the Apostle understood so little His spirit and teaching.

Notwithstanding their close and constant intimacy with the Divine Master, they utterly failed to understand and grasp His beautiful doctrine. They continued dull and blind, and were timid and full of fears.

Before dying, for instance, Our Lord told them in the clearest way that He would arise on the third day from the dead. So clear was this promise that His enemies understood it perfectly.

After Christ's death, they went to Pilate and said to him, "This imposter promised to rise from the dead on the third day, so place a guard of soldiers around the tomb lest His disciples steal the body and say that He has arisen. The last error will then be worse than the first."

Pilate fully understood them and at once sent a body of soldiers to guard the sepulchre.

Our Lord rose on the third day as He had promised, but the Apostles never even thought of it!

Mary Magdalen, so loving and faithful, went on the third day to anoint Our Lord's body, as was the custom of the Jews. When she did not find the body in the tomb, she thought that someone had stolen it, never dreaming that Christ had arisen.

Then it was that Our Lord revealed Himself to her and bade her tell the Apostles. Afterwards He appeared to them Himself and upbraided them for their want of faith.

St. Thomas, who was not with them, refused to believe that they had seen Him, saying, "Unless I place my finger in the wounds of His hands and my hand in the wound of His side I will not believe."

After they had seen Him go up to Heaven they were still weak and full of fear.

When Did They Understand?

When, however, the Holy Ghost descended upon them at Pentecost, they were at once changed. In an instant, the Holy Ghost made them understand all that Jesus had been teaching them for three years but which they had failed to grasp. All their fears vanished, and they went into the midst of their enemies preaching Jesus Christ.

They then divided the whole world among themselves, preaching the Gospel, casting down the false idols, and planting the doctrine of Christ in their place.

They did not fear the Roman emperors, nor the proud philosophers of Greece and Rome, whom they confounded.

What happened to the Apostles is still happening to all those who do not know and love the Holy Ghost. They are blind and cannot see. Their ideas are vague and erroneous. They must begin at once to love and pray to the Holy Ghost.

The Story of the Martyrs

Not only the Apostles, but all Christians who love and pray to the Holy Ghost receive the light, the strength, the help to do everything that they are called upon to do.

In the first centuries of the Church, Christians were persecuted most cruelly. They were subjected to many and excruciating tortures in order to compel them to deny their faith and adore the pagan idols.

How was it that they were able to endure those torments, the very thought of which makes us shudder? Some, after their flesh had been torn to pieces with whips and iron hooks, were placed on a slow fire like **St. Lawrence** who, after being roasted on one side, said to the executioners, "Now that I am roasted on the right side, turn me onto the left."

The Holy Ghost not only gave them courage and strength to bear the most cruel tortures, but enabled them to answer the most subtle arguments of their persecutors.

"Be not solicitous how or what you shall answer, or what you shall say; for the Holy Ghost shall teach you in the same hour what you must say." (*Luke* 12:11–12).

The young maiden **St. Lucy,** when summoned before a cruel judge and commanded to deny her faith, answered his arguments with such clearness that all who heard her were amazed.

Seeing their surprise, she said to them, "It is not

I but the Holy Ghost, who is in me and in all who lead chaste and holy lives, who enables me to answer you."

Then the brutal judge said, "We will rob you of your chastity, and then the Holy Ghost will not be with you."

But God did not allow them to harm her. The united strength of her fierce executioners failed to move her from the spot where she stood.

Similar things happened to **St. Agnes, St. Cecilia, St. Philomena** and hosts of other young maidens— to boys, old men and women of all classes and ages.

At all times the Church has been attacked and the Christians subjected—now in one country, now in another—to barbarous tortures. This has happened in our own days in Spain during the Red War when many bishops, thousands of priests, nuns, and young girls were subjected to the most appalling sufferings, which they bore with unflinching courage and constancy, so that the Holy Father declared them to be equal to the early martyrs.

Similar atrocities are being committed at present in several countries of the world, and the Holy Ghost is giving the poor victims strength to bear them.

Missionaries

In every century, too, priests and nuns have, like the Apostles, evangelized vast territories and converted millions to the faith of Jesus Christ.

St. Hyacinth, for example, the famous Dominican missionary, brought to the Church so many millions of pagans that it would appear incredible had we not most certain proof of what he did.

The wonders worked by **St. Vincent Ferrer** are no less surprising. In the Bull of his canonization, 873 great miracles wrought by him are mentioned. He converted 80,000 Jews, 70,000 Moslems and an incredibly great number of the most hardened sinners.

In more recent times, **Lord Salisbury,** Prime Minister of England, received some missionaries and nuns who were going to a distant part of the British Empire.

He asked how they hoped to live amidst such fierce tribes. "Why," he said, "you haven't a single gun nor any other means of defense"—to which they replied, "God will help and defend us." Lord Salisbury did not conceal his surprise.

Inspired and strengthened by the Holy Ghost, young ladies of the best families, delicately nurtured and surrounded with every home comfort, joyfully abandon this happiness to devote themselves to educate the young, to nurse the sick, to help the poor, to care for the blind, the deaf, the dumb and the insane.

Others fear not to go to far distant lands, without hope of return, and consecrate themselves to every form of charity and good works in favor of the heathens.

Chapter 8

The Wonderful Graces We Receive from the Holy Ghost

What we wish above all to make clear is that the Holy Ghost does not only give His wonderful help to Apostles, to martyrs, to missionaries, but to *all Christians without exception*, if only they ask Him as they should. This many fail to do—with the saddest consequences.

The happiness of our lives depends on choosing the proper state in life. If we follow the vocation God wishes us to follow, we have a guarantee of success. God gives us graces for every step of the road He has marked out for us. These graces we do not receive if we choose a manner of life different from what God has chosen for us.

How are we to know what He wills us to do? Simply by praying earnestly to the Holy Ghost for light and guidance.

This applies very especially to girls and boys when beginning life. If a boy, called on by God to become a priest, or a girl to become a nun, choose instead a secular life, they cannot expect God's help on the wrong way they are following. One reason why so many marriages are unhappy is that boys and girls, never intended by God to marry, blindly follow their own caprice and choose the married state.

* **Boys and girls** should earnestly ask God to manifest to them His Holy Will in this most important step of their lives. They should know if they ought to marry or not. They must ask God also, in case He wishes them to marry, to help them choose the proper partner, for this also is a frequent cause of unhappy marriages, *viz.*, marrying the wrong person.

Parents have the greatest responsibility in the education of their children. They are to blame countless times for the faults and unhappiness of their boys and girls, and many times for the loss of their children's souls.

Once more, the reason is that parents do not think of asking the Holy Ghost to enlighten them in this grave responsibility.

Businessmen frequently embark on serious enterprises never dreaming of or seeking the guidance of the Holy Ghost. Hence, so many failures,

The following incident, one of the many we might quote, shows how true this is.

Two merchants in the city of Lyons, engaged in the same line of business, had their establishments on the same street.

Both worked hard, both were shrewd businessmen, but whereas one prospered, the other lost heavily.

This latter, confiding in his more prosperous rival, explained his difficulties and asked his advice.

"My dear friend," was the reply, "you are fully as clever and keen as I am, and it seems to me that you work even harder. I attribute all my success to the fact that I hear Mass daily and ask for the guidance of the Holy Ghost. Do the same and you will succeed."

Surprised and disappointed at this answer, the less fortunate merchant returned to his home and related the fact to his wife. She gave him the sage advice to follow his friend's counsel. This he did, with the happiest results.

Professional men in every branch of life succeed marvellously in their various callings if they pray earnestly to the Holy Ghost.

Eminent doctors hear Mass and receive Holy Communion before performing important operations. This they do to ask God's help.

The ablest statesmen attribute their success to the guidance of the Holy Ghost, whose help they invoke.

St. Louis, King of France, who labored perhaps more strenuously than any man in his kingdom and who was one of the best and most glorious sovereigns who ever ruled over France, found time to hear two or three Masses every day.

Some of the courtiers suggested that he was overtaxing himself with so many Masses. The King replied: "You forget, my good friends, that by hearing Mass I confer the most important benefits on my Kingdom, many more than I could possibly do in any other way."

Salazar, the Prime Minister of Portugal, who has done prodigies in the uplifting of his country, is a devout Catholic and places his trust in God's help.

General Franco, who has not only saved Spain from the gravest crisis in her history but who has helped to save Europe from ruin, is known to spend long hours of the night praying before the Blessed Sacrament when faced with grave difficulties.

Mr. de Valera, the Irish Premier, hears Mass and receives Holy Communion daily. He too is a distinguished statesman and has succeeded in doing great things for his country.

The bravest and most successful generals have had recourse to God for help and light to gain their victories.

At Valverde, the celebrated Portuguese general—one of the greatest of his day—**Nuno Alvares Pereira,** was trapped and surrounded by immensely superior forces of the enemy, who while holding him on lower ground, occupied the vantage points on surrounding hills. All seemed irremediably lost. Advance meant death, retreat was impossible, surrender, he would not think of.

In the midst of the battle, when the contest was fiercest, the Portuguese commander fell on his knees. In answer to the cries of his captains who conjured him to get up and save them, he calmly replied:

"My friends, let me finish my prayers." Then, rising as a man inspired, imbued with a new vigor and courage, he leaped on his horse, shouted his battle cry, and pointing to the very center of the enemy lines, he led the attack. Small in stature but herculean in strength, he hewed down with his own hands the leaders of the enemy. The conflict was rude, but the battle was won.

This great general heard three Masses every day and obliged his men to hear one, and this, even during his constant campaigns, for he had ever care to have priests with his army.

The famous general and hero, **Simon de Montfort,** with only eight hundred horse soldiers and very few foot soldiers, was unexpectedly surrounded in the town of Muret by an enemy army of 40,000 men, led by the King of Aragon and Raymond, the Count of Toulouse. He sought help from God and was hearing Mass when his officers came to announce that the besieging army was marching to attack the town.

"Let me finish the Mass first," he replied, "and then I will be with you."

Full of trust, he ordered the gates to be flung open, and he charged right at the heart of the approaching army, threw it into utter disorder, struck down the King of Aragon himself, and won a glorious victory.

Emperor Lothaire heard three Masses every day, even when he was on the battlefield with his troops.

A notable case in modern times was that of the French **Marshal Foch,** who heard Mass every morning, even when the fighting was fiercest.

On one occasion, when the Prime Minister went to consult him on a matter of grave military importance, he was informed that the Marshal was hearing Mass. The aide-de-camp suggested calling him. "No, no," replied the Prime Minister, "we must not disturb him in his devotions. I will wait."

As we have already said, it is by prayer, by receiving the Sacraments and by hearing Holy Mass that we receive the graces and blessings of the Holy Ghost, His light, His guidance and His help.

Chapter 9

What We Lose by Not Loving the Holy Ghost

Owing to their ignorance of the Holy Ghost, many Catholics remain cold and tepid all their lives and never enjoy the religion of peace and love that Christ gave us.

For instance, **Holy Communion,** with all its immense joys, is by many little understood and little loved. They receive it but do not enjoy it, nor do they know what oceans of graces they could get in every Communion. Therefore, they receive Holy Communion coldly and seldom.

In Communion, it is God Himself, the Great Creator, the Omnipotent God, who comes into our souls. He comes with infinite love. He remains in us as long as the Sacred Host retains the appearance of bread. That may be for a long time. Oh, what precious moments!

He comes into us with infinite love and unites Himself so intimately with our soul that He becomes one with us.

One Communion is sufficient to make us Saints. **Little Imelda** became a Saint by one Holy Communion, simply because, with the light of the Holy

Ghost, she understood the wonders of Communion. We do not understand Holy Communion because we do not ask the Holy Ghost to give us His light, which He would most certainly do if we only asked Him.

All eternity will not be sufficient to thank God for one Holy Communion. **Zaccheus,** the publican and the sinner, received Our Lord once into his house, and that one visit made him a Saint. Our Lord comes, *not* into our houses, but into our very souls, not once, but many times, and we derive but little benefit from His visits; whereas, one Communion, as we have said, is enough to make a Saint.

Mary Magdalen and **Martha** were filled with joy when Jesus visited them in their home in Bethany. We should enjoy Our Lord's visit as they did, but, far from it, many swallow the Sacred Host and at once begin to read their prayerbooks.

We can well understand the joy and delight of St. Catherine of Siena, St. Rose of Lima, St. Anthony and other Saints when Our Lord appeared and spoke lovingly to them in their rooms, as He often did.

In Communion, He does much more for us. He comes really and truly into our souls, with a most tender love.

Oh, what graces could we not receive if only we asked for light from the Holy Ghost!

Then there is the Real Presence of Our Lord in the Blessed Sacrament, where He is waiting for us, ready to hear our prayers and give us every grace. Yet, many Catholics rarely or never visit Him, although they pass the church door frequently. They have difficulties and they have sorrows. They seek help and consolation from others, who cannot give it. Why do they not go to Our Lord and ask Him for help? When on earth, He consoled and comforted all who went to Him. He is here too on a throne of mercy. It is incalculable what graces we could receive in one short visit to the Blessed Sacrament. Yet the churches are for the greater part of the day almost empty.

It is true that some *do* understand this mystery of love. There are many doctors, lawyers, businessmen, pious women who pay two or four visits every day to the Blessed Sacrament on their way to or from business. This shows that others could do the same.

Protestants and unbelievers are naturally surprised and ask: "If you believe that your God, a God of infinite Goodness, is on the altar waiting for you, why don't you go to see Him and pray to Him?"

It seems incredible that Catholics do not open their eyes to the fact that God is really there waiting for them. The reason is that they do not pray to the Holy Ghost.

St. Teresa, after death, appeared to one of her nuns and said: "You ought to do before the Blessed Sacrament what we do in Heaven, for it is the very same God that you have on the altar that we have in Heaven."

Next, there is the great Sacrifice of the Mass, which is in every way equal to the death of Christ on the Cross. Every Mass brings oceans of graces to the Earth, but especially, to those who assist at it. There is nothing on earth equal to the Mass, and nothing in Heaven greater. Multitudes of angels assist at every Mass and gladly offer our prayers to God, thereby giving our petitions a marvelous efficacy. Everyone would like to see a miracle. Above all, one would like to see a dead man raised to life. That, indeed, would be a wonder that one could never forget.

But in every Mass a far greater wonder is wrought. The priest does much more than raise a dead man to life; he transforms the little host into the Body and Blood of the Son of God Himself. We can say that Jesus is born and Jesus dies in the Mass for love of us.

Notwithstanding this, many Catholics fail to assist at Mass. It is celebrated at a short distance from their homes, but they are too lazy, too careless to get up and assist at it.

Oh, did they know the immense graces and favors they receive at every Mass, they would hear not one, but many Masses every day! We ask again, "What is the cause of their blindness?" It is always the same, *viz.*, they do not pray to the Holy Ghost.

Prayer. There is nothing easier, nothing more consoling than prayer. It is easier to pray well than to pray badly. All that is necessary is to *know how to pray*. The whole secret is that when we pray we are talking to God personally and intimately. He is looking at us lovingly, listening to us, ready to give us everything. Let us understand once and for all that when praying we are in God's very presence.

This is not a metaphor or a way of speaking. It is the plain truth. Those who pray this way get more by one prayer than others by a hundred. Who would not like to talk to God, to a God who is so good, who is ready to give us everything? If we only asked the Holy Ghost, He would teach us how to grasp this truth.

All these wonderful graces, joys and consolations we lose by our want of love for the Holy Ghost.

The Love of God

The greatest of all our obligations, the greatest source of merit, our greatest possible consolation is to love God. One act of love is worth a thousand acts of any other virtue. No work, however important, is worth anything unless it be inspired by love of God.

The First Great Commandment is to love God with all our heart and soul. It is the basis and the very essence of our religion.

Yet many Christians have little or no love of God. They find no consolation in making acts of love. They tell us themselves that when they repeat an act of love, they feel nothing in their hearts corresponding to the words.

They adore God, they serve God, they pray to God, they fear God. Their idea of God is false; they think of Him as a severe God, a stern God, but do not think of Him as a God of infinite love, sweetness and mercy.

As a consequence, they fail to get the immense merits they could so easily get in their daily lives, they never enjoy the friendship of God which would be their supreme happiness.

God has done everything to make us love Him. He commands us to call Him Father, that is, Father in the truest sense of the word, the most loving, tender Father.

God has made, as He tells us Himself, the last supreme effort to gain our love, by offering us His Sacred Heart as the emblem, the pledge of His most tender love for us.

He has made 12 most loving promises to all who are devout to His Sacred Heart, but few, indeed, ever think of these wonderful promises.

How is it that we are so blind, so cold, so unloving? It is always the same answer, *viz.*: we do not ask the Holy Ghost for His Light.

The Passion

One of the greatest losses we suffer by not being devoted to the Holy Ghost is our incredible blindness regarding the Great Mystery of the Passion.

Our Lord suffered the most ignominious and cruel death to save us. He could have saved us with one word or with one drop of His Precious Blood. Why did He submit Himself to such outrages, blasphemies and insults?

Simply to compel us to love Him, to prove to us in the clearest possible way how much He loved us.

He died not for all in general. He died for each one of us in particular. He saw you, dear Reader, clearly and distinctly, and offered every pang of pain, every drop of His Precious Blood for you.

And yet, knowing all this, we look on the Crucifix, we look on the representations of the Passion and yet feel no love for the God who suffered so much for us; we feel no gratitude. We remain cold, unmoved, unresponsive.

We do not here speak of mere emotional love, but of a clear intellectual understanding of God's love which He showed by His sufferings and death.

Why is it that we do not grasp this Great Mystery? It is because we have not the light of the Holy Ghost.

All the Saints were Saints because they understood the Passion, and there was never a Saint who did not love and was not grateful to Our Lord for suffering for us. It is not possible to understand this Divine Proof of love and not love back.

Let us then beg and implore the Holy Ghost to help us to understand the infinite love of Our Lord for us in the Passion.

Chapter 10

The Three Sacraments
Of the Holy Ghost

We receive, as already said, by prayer, good works and the Sacraments, an increase of the gifts and graces of the Holy Spirit, but there are three Sacraments which we might call Sacraments of the Holy Ghost, *viz.*, Baptism, Confirmation and Confession.

Baptism

The Holy Ghost does not come into our souls personally when we are created, nor when we are born into this world, *but when we are baptized.*

In Baptism our souls are purified from the horrible leprosy of Original Sin and clothed with Sanctifying Grace, of which we have just spoken. It is in Baptism that the Holy Ghost enters *personally* and takes up His *residence* in our souls, and makes them His living temples.

How foolish, then, are the parents who defer the Baptism of their children! They are depriving them of the loving presence and protection of the Holy Ghost. The life of a child is so frail that it may die at any moment. How awful if the child were to die and be deprived forever of seeing God, of going to Heaven!

The writer of these lines had once the sadness of seeing a little child die thus suddenly. The fact is worth narrating.

A priest was asked to baptize the child, which he gladly consented to do. Days passed and the Baptism did not take place. Retiring to rest one night, the thought flashed across his mind of the danger of the child's dying. He had no especial reason for his fear, but acting on the inspiration, he insisted the next day on the Baptism being performed at once. This was done, fortunately, and not a day too soon, for the child died unexpectedly from a sudden fit of convulsions.

Unfortunately, many children do die unexpectedly without Baptism. What a dreadful responsibility for the parents!

Confirmation

Confirmation is in a most special way the Sacrament of the Holy Ghost, for though He comes into our souls in Baptism and makes them His living temples, it is in Confirmation that we receive Him in all His plenitude.

The Apostles had received Him, too, before Our Lord went up to Heaven, for He had said to them: "Receive ye the Holy Ghost. Whose sins you shall forgive, they are forgiven; whose sins you shall retain, they are retained," but as we saw, it was at Pentecost that they received Him in all His fullness.

This Sacrament is of most vital importance and can only be received once. Therefore, every care should be taken to make due preparation for its reception.

As a rule, care is taken that boys and girls who are to be confirmed know their Catechism. But, incredibly, many times they are taught very little, or nothing at all, about the Holy Ghost Himself! They are not taught how to love and honor Him. They do not know the wonderful graces He gives them. They seldom or never pray to Him.

As a consequence, they do not receive Confirmation with that joy and delight with which they receive their First Communion. Still worse, during all their life after they do not cherish the love and devotion they ought to for the Holy Ghost. They are thus deprived of the immense help and consolations they should enjoy.

Teachers are responsible for this neglect. They themselves seem to know little about the Holy Ghost. It is the case of the blind leading the blind.

Dear Teachers who read these lines, strive to teach your students henceforth to love the Holy Ghost.

Confession

Confession, too, is in a special way a Sacrament of the Holy Ghost.

It is a wonderful Sacrament and is a very river of graces.

a) Only God can forgive sin, for it demands an omnipotent, divine power. The highest angels in Heaven cannot forgive a single sin. The Holy Ghost gives this divine power to priests, to whom He says: "Receive ye the Holy Ghost; whose sins you shall forgive, they are forgiven."

St. Augustine says that when a priest forgives a sin, he uses a power greater than the power God Himself used in creating the world. In proportion to this divine power are the graces given in Confession.

b) Yet another fact: If anyone should commit a mortal sin and so expel the Holy Ghost from his soul, Confession purifies the soul in the Blood of Jesus Christ and brings back the Holy Ghost, who once more comes to dwell in the soul as in His Temple and gives it again all His gifts and graces.

Many people come to Confession in the most casual, offhand way. They have venial and mortal sins on their souls but do not realize the awful malice and filth of those sins. Did they see their souls in the state of sin, they would die of horror.

Cardinal Newman observes that were we to see a body in an advanced state of corruption, the stench and appearance of it would fill us with horror and disgust. Yet such corruption is nothing in comparison with that of a soul in sin.

To show how true this is, a venial sin may detain

a soul in the awful fires of Purgatory for a long time. A mortal sin detains a soul in Hell forever and ever. These sins, therefore, must be very dreadful to deserve such awful punishment.

God does not punish a sin simply because He is angry, but because the malice of sin demands that punishment. So true is this that, were a soul to enter Heaven in the state of venial sin, it would of its own accord hurl itself into the fires of Purgatory, to be there cleansed from that sin.

Notwithstanding this, people come to Confession with but little sorrow and compunction and scarcely thank God for cleansing them from this hideous corruption.

When Our Lord cured the ten lepers of their awful disease, only one came back to thank Him. We are justly indignant at such vile ingratitude, yet many of us are far more ungrateful, for we thank God so little for curing us of the leprosy of sin, which is incomparably more vile.

The malice of sin is dreadful; the corruption, the filth of sin is awful; but there is something far, far worse, and that is that sin is a direct, personal offense and outrage to the Majesty of God.

Few Catholics think of this. The consequence is that their sorrow for sin is but little and their resolution to avoid sin is far from being as firm and sincere as it ought to be. They do not make proper preparation for Confession. Therefore, they do not receive in their Confessions the wonderful graces that they should receive.

Some Catholics fail to derive the consolation and help from Confession that they should. Our Blessed Lord in Confession gives us a friend to whom we can declare all our troubles and who is ready to console and comfort all who kneel at his feet. He has been prepared by many years' study for this all-important part of his mission. He does not give his opinions, but the doctrine of the Church and the counsels of the Saints, and he is, moreover, helped and inspired by the Holy Ghost, whose minister he is.

Penitents do well to listen to his counsels and put them into practice. They should ask advice in their doubts and difficulties. Strange to say, Protestants sometimes seem to understand this part of Confession better than Catholics, and, moreover, some enter the Catholic Church expressly that they may be able to go to Confession!

The reason is that these Catholics have not the light of the Holy Ghost. They do not love and they do not pray to the Holy Ghost.

Chapter 11

Sins Against the Holy Ghost

The following words of Our Lord show how grievous are sins against the Holy Ghost: "Every sin and blasphemy shall be forgiven men, but the blasphemy of the Spirit shall not be forgiven."

The sins against the Holy Ghost are commonly said to be six, *viz.*, **despair, presumption, impenitence, obstinacy, resisting truth,** and **envy of another's spiritual welfare.**

Some of these are less difficult of pardon than others. Final impenitence is absolutely unpardonable. Those, too, who from deliberate malice refuse to recognize the work of God, as the Pharisees did when they saw the miracles of Our Lord and attributed them to Beelzebub, the Prince of Devils [are unpardonable].

Those who reject deliberately the means of salvation are also rarely pardoned.

The difficulty in obtaining pardon for these sins is clearly caused by the sinner himself, who rejects God's grace.

Deliberate and habitual sins, sins against the light

[of truth], offend God more gravely than sins due to weakness and ignorance.

The Great Sin Against the Holy Ghost and Its Punishment

The fall of Constantinople and its destruction is a striking example of the awful punishment meted out by God to those who sin against the Holy Spirit.

The Greeks, led by their Patriarchs Photius and Cerularius, denied the divinity of the Holy Ghost and, after apparently renouncing their error, fell back into the same sin. They were threatened by Pope Nicholas V with God's anger if they did not repent. This they obstinately refused to do.

Three years later, in 1453, Mahomet II, at the head of a formidable Moslem army, surrounded the city and after fierce fighting defeated the Greeks and captured Constantinople—this, on the very feast of the Holy Ghost. Fearful massacres, pillage and fires lasted three whole days, reducing the inhabitants to an awful plight. Mahomet, on the fourth day, entered the city, took possession of the Imperial Palace and turned the cathedral into a mosque.

Constantinople has since then lain under the cruel yoke of the Turks for over *500 years*. What a punishment!

What about Ourselves?

Do we offend the Holy Ghost? *Do we* sin against the Holy Ghost?

Let us hope that we never sin as gravely as those who do not deserve pardon, but perhaps for want of thought we offend our Divine Guest by lesser sins.

The Holy Ghost loves us with an infinitely tender and divine love. He loves us so dearly that He actually comes, as we have said, and remains in our souls. We are, therefore, bound to return this Divine love.

Do we do so, or, like so many faithless ones, do we forget Him, abandon Him and pay no heed to Him?

Or worse still, do we dare offend Him to His very face? If so, we must earnestly try to correct these faults. Here are some useful suggestions.

A pagan philosopher gave this wise advice to a disciple who asked him how best he could correct his faults.

"Think," answered Seneca, "that you are in the company of a good man who sees what you are doing and hears what you say. Do nothing that you would not do in his presence."

Following this counsel, the disciple soon corrected his faults.

St. Bernard gave similar advice to his monks: "Do nothing," he said to them, "that you would not do if I were present."

No thief, however daring he may be, will steal if he sees a policeman looking at him.

If then we realize that the Holy Ghost Himself is really and truly with us and sees all we do, it will be a powerful incentive to avoid offending Him.

The following little fact will serve as an example:

A young lady on her birthday received from her mother a most beautiful and costly dress. She hastily ran up to her room and donned the new frock, with which she was delighted.

Suddenly, a wave of sadness took the place of her joy, and going to her mother, she said with tears in her eyes: "Mother, I cannot wear this dress. It is not modest. The Holy Ghost, who is in my soul, would be displeased."

This young girl teaches us all an important lesson, for if we too have a clear idea, as she had, that the Holy Ghost is in us, we shall avoid all words and acts that offend Him.

Veni Creator Spiritus

Come, O Creator Spirit blest,
And in our souls take up Thy rest;
Come with Thy grace and heavenly aid,
To fill the hearts which Thou hast made.

Great Paraclete, to Thee we cry,
O highest Gift of God most high!

O Fount of life, O Fire of love!
And sweet Anointing from above!

Thou in Thy sevenfold gifts art known;
The finger of God's hand, we own,
The promise of the Father, Thou!
Who dost the tongue with pow'r endow.

Kindle our senses from above,
And make our hearts o'erflow with love;
With patience firm and virtue high,
The weakness of our flesh supply.

Far from us drive the foe we dread,
And grant us Thy true peace instead;
So shall we not with Thee for guide
Turn from the path of life aside.

Oh, may Thy grace on us bestow
The Father and the Son to know!
And Thee through endless time confess'd
Of both th' eternal Spirit blest.

All glory while the ages run
Be to the Father and the Son
Who rose from death; the same to Thee,
O Holy Ghost, eternally!   Amen.

Prayers to the Holy Ghost

Litany of the Holy Ghost
(For private use only.)

Lord, have mercy on us.
  Christ, have mercy on us.
Lord, have mercy on us. Father all powerful,
  Have mercy on us.
Jesus, Eternal Son of the Father, Redeemer of the
  world, *Save us.*
Spirit of the Father and the Son, boundless Life of
  both, *Sanctify us.*
Holy Trinity, *Hear us.*

Holy Ghost, Who proceedest from the Father
  and the Son, *enter our hearts.*
Holy Ghost, Who art equal to the Father and
  the Son, *enter our hearts.*
Promise of God the Father, *have mercy on us.*
Ray of heavenly light, *have mercy on us.*
Author of all good, *etc.*
Source of heavenly water,

---

*Added by the Publisher to the 1991 edition.

Consuming Fire,
Ardent Charity,
Spiritual Unction,
Spirit of love and truth,
Spirit of wisdom and understanding,
Spirit of counsel and fortitude,
Spirit of knowledge and piety,
Spirit of the fear of the Lord,
Spirit of grace and prayer,
Spirit of peace and meekness,
Spirit of modesty and innocence,
Holy Ghost, the Comforter,
Holy Ghost, the Sanctifier,
Holy Ghost, Who governest the Church,
Gift of God the Most High,
Spirit Who fillest the universe,
Spirit of the adoption of the children of God,

Holy Ghost, *inspire us with horror of sin.*
Holy Ghost, *come and renew the face of the earth.*
Holy Ghost, *shed Thy light into our souls.*
Holy Ghost, *engrave Thy law in our hearts.*
Holy Ghost, *inflame us with the flame of Thy love.*
Holy Ghost, *open to us the treasures of Thy graces.*
Holy Ghost, *teach us to pray well.*
Holy Ghost, *enlighten us with Thy heavenly inspirations.*
Holy Ghost, *lead us in the way of salvation.*
Holy Ghost, *grant us the only necessary knowledge.*
Holy Ghost, *inspire in us the practice of good.*

Holy Ghost, *grant us the merits of all virtues*.
Holy Ghost, *make us persevere in justice*.
Holy Ghost, *be Thou our everlasting reward*.

Lamb of God, Who takest away the sins of the world,
   Send us Thy Holy Ghost.
Lamb of God, Who takest away the sins of the world,
   *Pour down into our souls the gifts of the Holy
   Ghost*.
Lamb of God, Who takest away the sins of the world,
   Grant us the Spirit of wisdom and piety.

V. Come, Holy Ghost! Fill the hearts of Thy
   faithful,
R. *And enkindle in them the fire of Thy love*.

LET US PRAY
Grant, O merciful Father, that Thy Divine Spirit
may enlighten, inflame and purify us, that He may
penetrate us with His heavenly dew and make us fruit-
ful in good works, through Our Lord Jesus Christ,
Thy Son, Who with Thee, in the unity of the same
Spirit, liveth and reigneth forever and ever. R. *Amen*.

A Novena Prayer to the
Holy Ghost for a Special Favor

O HOLY GHOST, Thou art the Third Person of
   the Blessed Trinity! Thou art the Spirit of truth,
love and holiness, proceeding from the Father and the
Son, and equal to Them in all things! I adore Thee

and love Thee with all my heart. Teach me to know and to seek God, by whom and for whom I was created. Fill my heart with a holy fear and a great love of Him. Give me compunction and patience, and do not let me fall into sin.

Increase in me faith, hope and charity, and bring forth in me all the virtues proper to my state of life. Help me to grow in the four cardinal virtues, Thy seven Gifts and Thy twelve Fruits.

Make me a faithful follower of Jesus Christ, an obedient child of the Church, and a help to my neighbor. Give me the grace to keep the Commandments and to receive the Sacraments worthily. Raise me to holiness in the state of life to which Thou hast called me, and lead me through a happy death to everlasting life, through Jesus Christ, our Lord.

Grant me also, O Holy Ghost, Giver of all good gifts, the special favor for which I ask (*name it*), if it be for Thy honor and glory and for my well-being.

Glory be to the Father and to the Son, and to the Holy Ghost, as it was in the beginning, is now, and ever shall be, world without end. Amen.

A Prayer for the Propagation Of the Catholic Faith

O HOLY SPIRIT, Spirit of truth, come into our hearts; shed the brightness of Thy light upon the nations, that they may please Thee in unity of faith. (From the *Raccolta*).

An Aspiration

O HOLY SPIRIT, sweet Guest of my soul, abide in me and grant that I may ever abide in Thee. (From the *Raccolta*).

A Prayer for the Church

O HOLY SPIRIT, Creator, mercifully assist Thy Catholic Church, and by Thy heavenly power strengthen and establish her against the assaults of all her enemies. By Thy love and grace renew the spirit of Thy servants whom Thou hast anointed, that in Thee they may glorify the Father and His only-begotten Son, Jesus Christ our Lord. Amen. (From the *Raccolta*).

Come, Holy Ghost

C OME, Holy Ghost, fill the hearts of Thy faithful, and kindle in them the fire of Thy love.

V. Send forth Thy Spirit, and they shall be created;
R. *And Thou shalt renew the face of the earth.*

LET US PRAY

O God, Who hast instructed the hearts of the faithful by the light of the Holy Ghost, grant that by the same Spirit we may be always truly wise, and ever rejoice in His consolation, through Christ our Lord. Amen. (From the *Roman Missal*).

A Daily Consecration to the Holy Ghost

MOST HOLY GHOST, receive the consecration that I make of my entire being. From this moment on, come into every area of my life and into each of my actions. Thou art my Light, my Guide, my Strength, and the sole desire of my heart. I abandon myself without reserve to Thy divine action, and I desire to be ever docile to Thine inspirations. O Holy Ghost, transform me, with and through Mary, into another Christ Jesus, for the glory of the Father and the salvation of the world. Amen. (*By the Servant of God, Fr. Felix de Jesus Rougier, M.Sp.S.*).

Prayer for the Seven Gifts Of the Holy Ghost

O LORD JESUS CHRIST, Who before ascending into Heaven didst promise to send the Holy Ghost to finish Thy work in the souls of Thine Apostles and Disciples, deign to grant the same Holy Spirit to me, that He may perfect in my soul the work of Thy grace and Thy love. Grant me the Spirit of Wisdom, that I may despise the perishable things of this world and aspire only after the things that are eternal; the Spirit of Understanding, to enlighten my mind with the light of Thy divine truth; the Spirit of Counsel, that I may ever choose the surest way of pleasing God and gaining Heaven;

the Spirit of Fortitude, that I may bear my cross with Thee and that I may overcome with courage all the obstacles that oppose my salvation; the Spirit of Knowledge, that I may know God and know myself and grow perfect in the science of the Saints; the Spirit of Piety, that I may find the service of God sweet and amiable; the Spirit of Fear, that I may be filled with a loving reverence towards God and may dread in any way to displease Him. Mark me, Dear Lord, with the sign of Thy true disciples, and animate me in all things with Thy Spirit. Amen.

Consecration to the Holy Ghost

O HOLY GHOST, divine Spirit of light and love, I consecrate to Thee my understanding, my heart and my will, my whole being, for time and eternity. May my understanding be always submissive to Thy heavenly inspirations and the teachings of the Catholic Church, of which Thou art the Infallible Guide. May my heart be ever inflamed with love of God and of my neighbor. May my will be ever conformed to the divine will, and may my whole life be a faithful imitation of the life and virtues of our Lord and Saviour Jesus Christ, to Whom, with the Father and Thee, be honor and glory forever. Amen.

An Act of Oblation to the Holy Spirit

ON MY KNEES before the great cloud of heavenly witnesses, I offer myself body and soul to Thee, eternal Spirit of God. I adore the brightness of Thy purity, the unerring keenness of Thy justice and the might of Thy love. Thou art the strength and light of my soul. In Thee I live and move and have my being. I desire never to grieve Thee by unfaithfulness to grace, and I pray with all my heart to be kept from the smallest sin against Thee. Make me faithful in every thought, and grant that I may always listen to Thy voice, watch for Thy light, and follow Thy gracious inspirations. I cling to Thee and give myself to Thee, and I ask Thee by Thy compassion to watch over me in my weakness. Holding the pierced feet of Jesus, looking at His five Wounds, trusting in His Precious Blood and adoring His opened side and stricken Heart, I implore Thee, adorable Spirit, Helper of my infirmity, so to keep me in Thy grace that I may never sin against Thee with the sin which Thou wilt not forgive. Grant to me the grace, O Holy Spirit, Spirit of the Father and of the Son, to say to Thee always and everywhere, "Speak, Lord, for Thy servant hears." Amen. (*After a prayer by Cardinal Newman*).